I0201591

Extreme Weather

Lucy Bashford

Explore other books at:
WWW.ENGAGEBOOKS.COM

VANCOUVER, B.C.

WWW.ENGAGEBOOKS.COM

Extreme Weather - Our Changing Planet: *Level 3*
Bashford, Lucy 1958 –
Text © 2023 Engage Books
Design © 2023 Engage Books

Edited by: A.R. Roumanis, Ashley Lee,
Melody Sun & Sarah Harvey
Design by: Rosie Gowsell Pattison

Text set in Arial Regular.
Chapter headings set in Arial Black.

FIRST EDITION / FIRST PRINTING

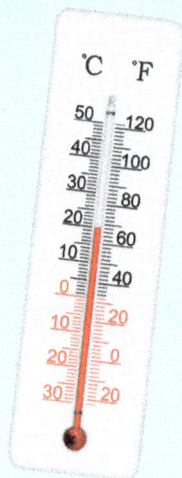

LIBRARY AND ARCHIVES CANADA CATALOGUING IN PUBLICATION

Extreme weather / Lucy Bashford.
Names: Bashford, Lucy, author.
Description: Series statement: Our changing planet

Identifiers: Canadiana (print) 20230159702 | Canadiana (ebook) 20230159710
ISBN 978-1-77476-895-2 (hardcover)
ISBN 978-1-77476-896-9 (softcover)
ISBN 978-1-77476-898-3 (pdf)
ISBN 978-1-77476-897-6 (epub)
ISBN 978-1-77878-123-0 (audio)

Subjects:
LCSH: Climatic extremes—Juvenile literature. |
LCSH: Climatic changes—Juvenile literature. |
LCSH: Severe storms—Juvenile literature. |
LCSH: Weather—Juvenile literature.

Classification: LCC QC981.8.C53 B37 2023 | DDC J363.34/92—DC23

This project has been made possible in part
by the Government of Canada.

Canada

Contents

What Is Extreme Weather?

Extreme **weather** can happen when normal weather patterns change. Extreme weather can be very hot or very cold. It can also be very wet or very dry. Strong storms are another kind of extreme weather. These events can be caused by nature or human activity.

KEY WORD

Weather: what the air and sky are like at a certain time. This includes wind, rain, or temperature.

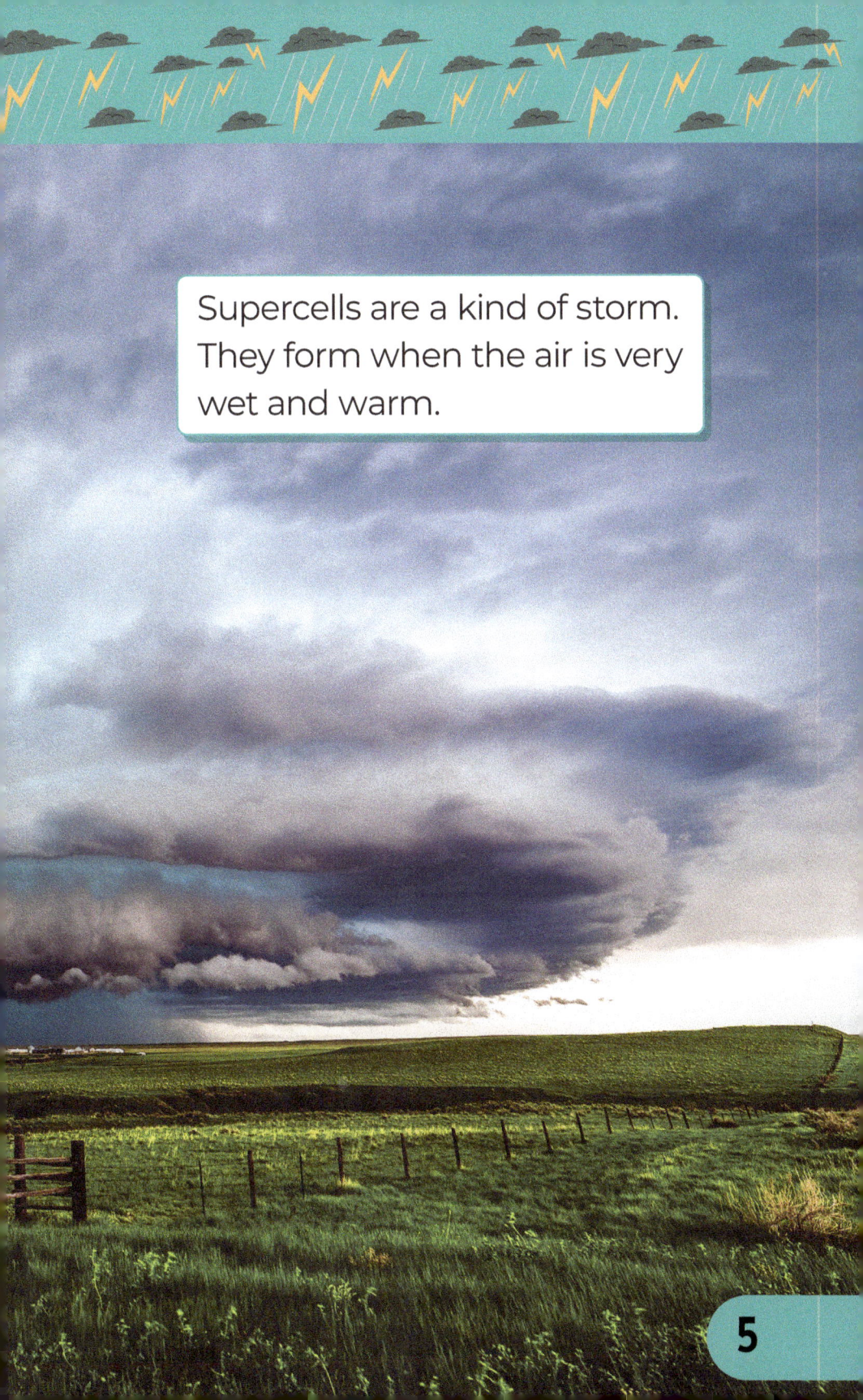

Supercells are a kind of storm. They form when the air is very wet and warm.

Extreme Weather: A Closer Look

During a heat wave, everything is dry. A lightning strike can start a wildfire. Heavy rainfall often causes flooding. Strong winds can create serious damage and injury.

Poor areas suffer the most. They do not have the money to rebuild their homes.

Extreme weather may last only a couple of days. It often goes on for longer. Cleaning up can take a lot of time.

Examples of Extreme Weather

Cyclones are storms that usually form over **tropical** waters. They bring heavy rain and cause sea levels to rise. They gather their energy from the surface of warm sea water. Wind speeds can go up to 150 miles (240 kilometers) per hour.

KEY WORD

Tropical: Areas that are hot with lots of rain year-round.

Cyclones are also called typhoons or hurricanes.

Tornadoes are fast spinning tubes of air that reach the ground. Another name for them is twisters. Their wind speeds range from 10 miles (16 km) per hour to 250 miles (402 km) per hour.

"Black blizzards" are dust storms that make day seem like night.

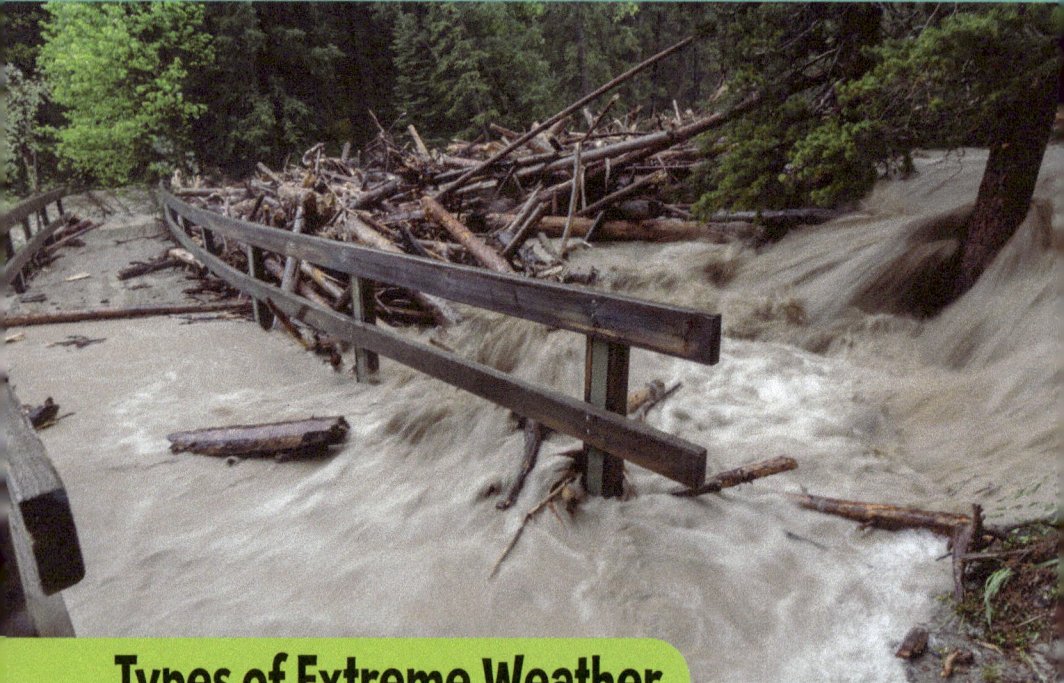

Types of Extreme Weather

Some extreme weather events are weather-related and others are related to **climate**. Weather events are short term. Heat waves, flash floods, or deep freezes do not last a long time.

KEY WORD

Climate: the weather in an area over a long period of time.

Climate events last longer. Some **droughts** last for years. Climate events also happen when there are many weather events over a long period of time.

KEY WORD

Droughts: long periods without rain.

Climate Change

Global temperatures are rising. This is causing Earth's climate to change. In the past, **climate change** happened slowly. Now it is speeding up.

Climate change: a change in the average temperature on Earth over a long period of time.

Since 1760, Earth's average temperature has gone up about 1.8° Fahrenheit (1° Celsius). By 2100, many scientists think that temperatures could go up another 3.6°F (2°C). This will cause more extreme weather events to happen.

Effects on the Planet

Extreme weather affects almost all life. Sometimes **ecosystems** do not recover. Some birds or plants may prefer the places they end up in after extreme weather. This is not always a good thing for that ecosystem.

KEY WORD

Ecosystems: areas where plants and animals live and interact.

Sea levels are rising because of global warming. There are two main reasons. Water is being added as huge masses of ice melt around the world. Also, sea water expands as it warms.

The island nation of Tuvalu may disappear because of rising sea levels.

Effects on Humans

Extreme weather affects people everywhere. Hurricanes damage towns and cities. Desert dust storms can reach hights of 20,000 feet (6,100 meters). These storms force people to leave their homes. They often do not have time to recover before the next storm.

People forced to leave their homes because of extreme weather are called climate refugees.

Extreme weather also affects people's health. These events make it easier for disease to spread. Higher temperatures and more rainfall can cause water to become dangerous to drink.

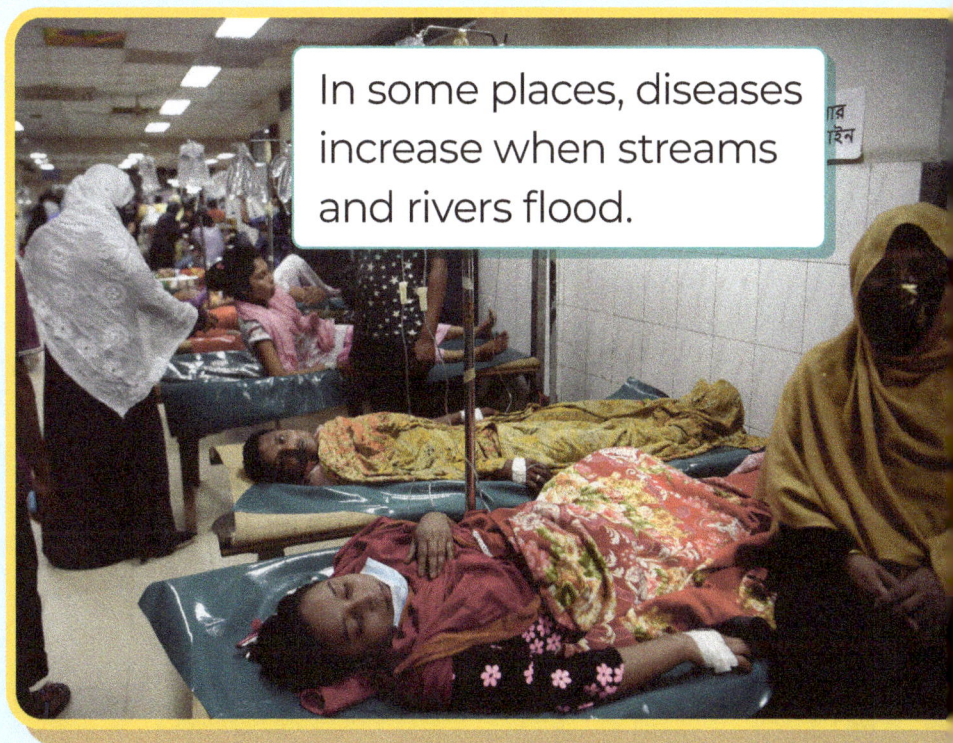

In some places, diseases increase when streams and rivers flood.

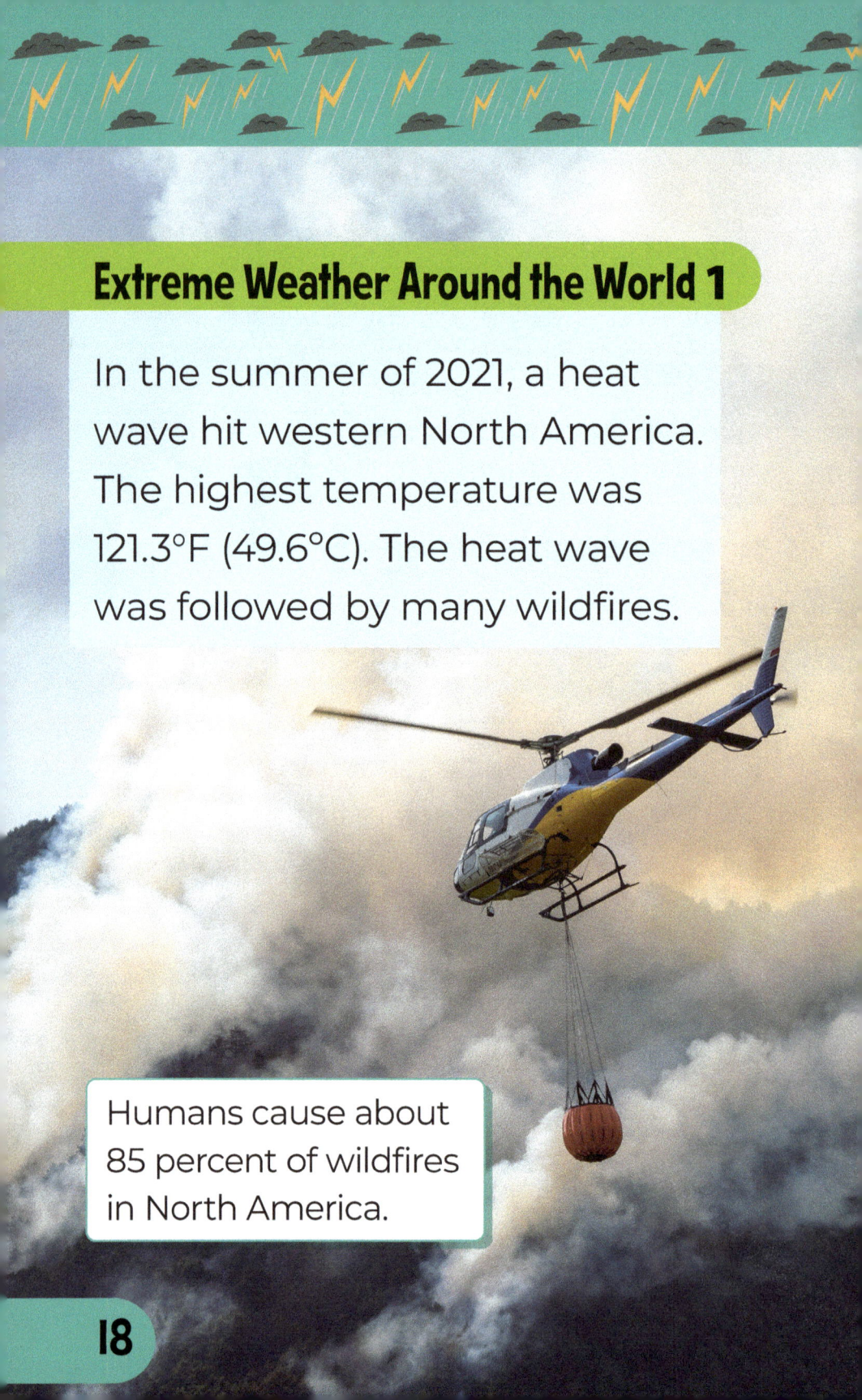

Extreme Weather Around the World 1

In the summer of 2021, a heat wave hit western North America. The highest temperature was 121.3°F (49.6°C). The heat wave was followed by many wildfires.

Humans cause about 85 percent of wildfires in North America.

In 2019, lightning strikes started intense bush fires in Australia. An area the size of South Korea burned. About three billion animals died or were injured. Many of these animals are found only in Australia.

More than 60,000 koala bears were harmed in the bush fires in Australia.

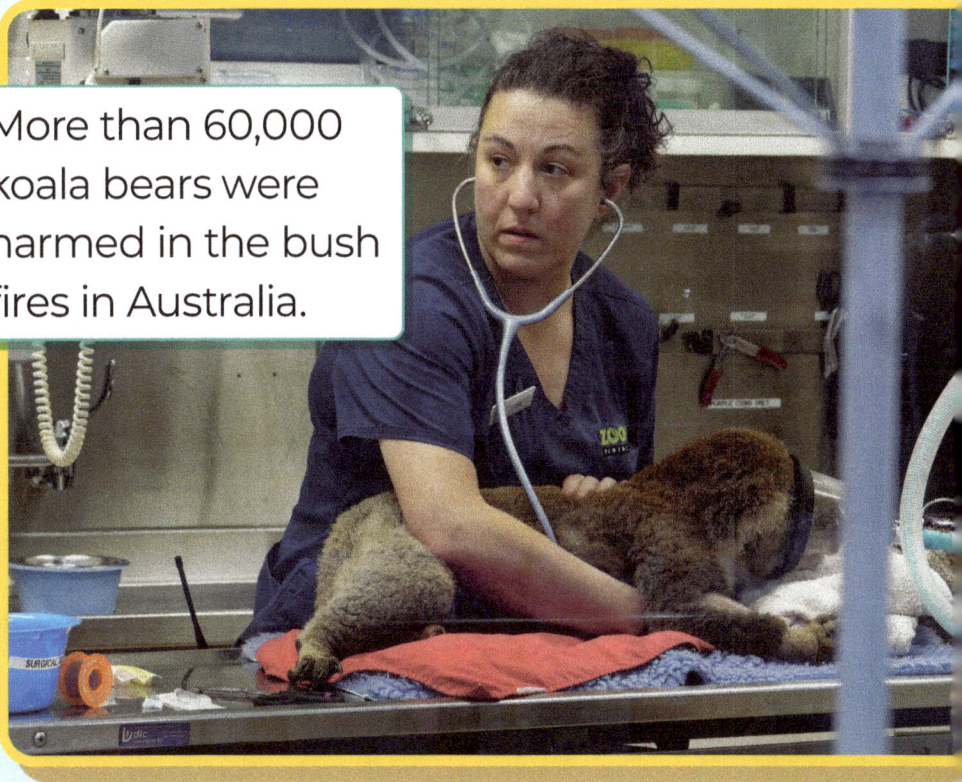

Extreme Weather Around the World 2

Eastern Africa had very little rain in 2022. The drought has **displaced** more than one million people. Many countries are sending food and medicine to help.

KEY WORD

Displaced: being forced to leave your home.

The Andes Mountains run through seven countries in South America. **Glaciers** in the Andes have shrunk by 30 percent. Lakes and rivers have dried up. The drought makes it difficult to grow food crops.

KEY WORD

Glaciers: huge masses of ice that form over many years.

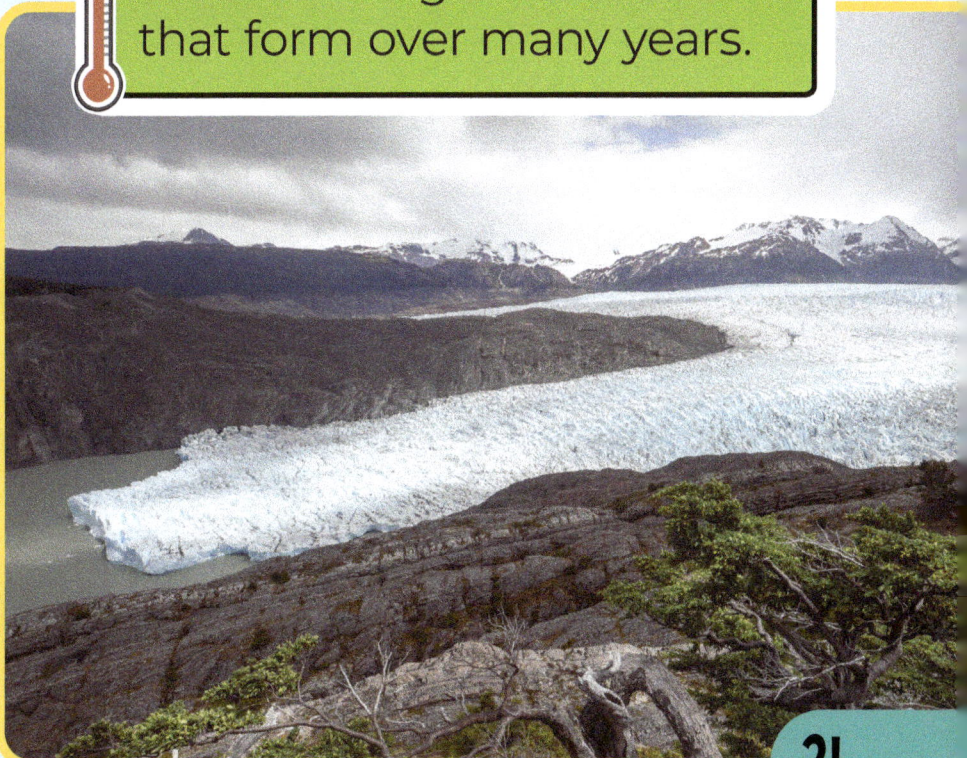

What Can Be Done About Extreme Weather?

Roads and bridges are being built to survive extreme weather. Houses can be built on land that is not at risk. This helps towns and cities stay safe and strong. But it does not stop extreme weather from happening.

Natural ecosystems need more time to adapt to change. Healthy forests soak up a **greenhouse gas** called carbon dioxide. This slowly helps lower Earth's temperature.

KEY WORD

Greenhouse gas: a gas that causes Earth to heat up.

Extreme Weather Solutions

Nature is helping seaside towns and cities adapt to extreme weather. Healthy kelp and seagrass beds can slow waves down. Mangrove forests help protect against soil **erosion**.

Mangrove roots grow along ocean and river shores.

KEY WORD

Erosion: when soil and rock are slowly removed by waves, rain, and wind.

Parks and green roofs help keep cities cool. Planting lots of trees creates shade. Trees also help keep stormwater under control by trapping water. This lowers the risk of flooding.

Builders are asked to set aside part of their roofs for plants in Toronto, Canada.

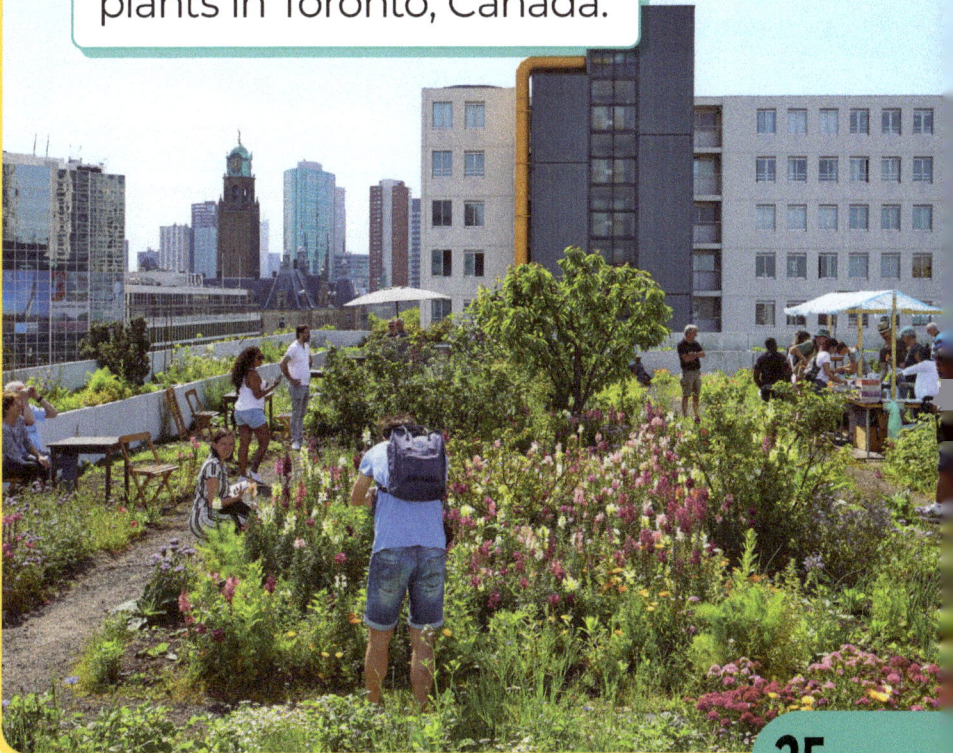

The Helpers 1

By changing human behavior, there can be fewer extreme weather events. Using more wind and solar power will help. So will cutting down the use of **fossil fuels**. This includes coal, oil, and natural gas.

KEY WORD

Fossil fuels: energy sources that can not be renewed.

Cities are building **reefs** using oyster shells and concrete. Baby oysters are placed on the reefs to grow. The reefs protect the shoreline from the erosion caused by waves.

The Helpers 2

Young people are asking governments to listen to scientists about climate change. Bill Nye is a scientist who is warning the world about global warming. He is asking people to use less fossil fuels. Bill Nye teaches kids that they can help to stop extreme weather.

Bill Nye joined the March for Science in 2017. He asked people to listen to scientists about climate change.

Young people lead climate action groups all over the world. Kids can share their creative ideas at the Youth UNESCO Climate Action Network (YoU-CAN). YoU-CAN helps young people start new projects that help Earth's climate. Look for climate action groups that you can join.

Quiz

Test your knowledge of extreme weather by answering the following questions. The questions are based on what you have read in this book. The answers are listed on the bottom of the next page.

1 Why does extreme weather happen?

2 What is the name for storms that make day seem like night?

3 Where do cyclones gather their energy?

4 What is causing extreme weather events to happen more often?

5 What are people called if they are forced to leave their homes because of extreme weather?

6 What is being used to build reefs that help protect shorelines?

Explore Other Level 3 Readers.

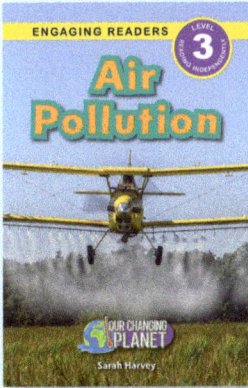

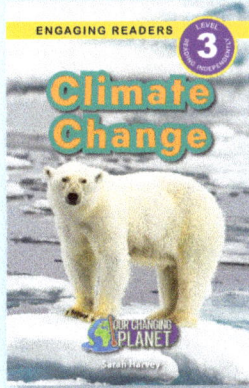

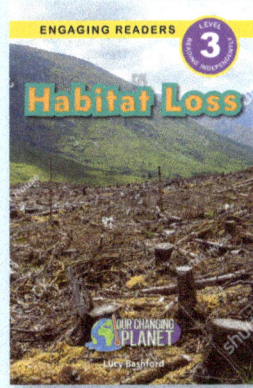

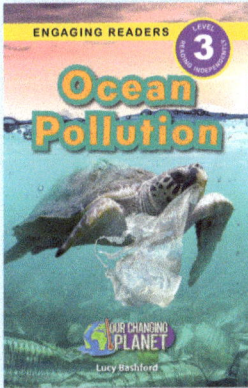

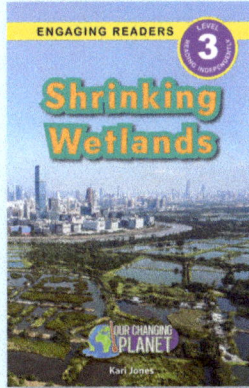

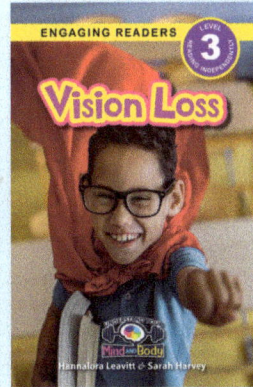

ENGAGING READERS — LEVEL 3

Air Pollution
Sarah Harvey
OUR CHANGING PLANET

Climate Change
Sarah Harvey
OUR CHANGING PLANET

Habitat Loss
Lucy Bashford
OUR CHANGING PLANET

Ocean Pollution
Lucy Bashford
OUR CHANGING PLANET

Shrinking Wetlands
Kari Jones
OUR CHANGING PLANET

Diabetes
Kit Caudron-Robinson
Understanding Your Mind and Body

Obesity
Kit Caudron-Robinson
Understanding Your Mind and Body

Autism
AJ Knight
Understanding Your Mind and Body

Vision Loss
Hannalora Leavitt & Sarah Harvey
Understanding Your Mind and Body

Visit www.engagebooks.com/readers

Answers: 1. When normal weather patterns change 2. Black blizzards 3. From the surface of warm sea water 4. Climate change 5. Climate refugees 6. Oysters and concrete

www.ingramcontent.com/pod-product-compliance
Lightning Source LLC
Chambersburg PA
CBHW051236020426

42331CB00016B/3398